BLACK ACHIEVEMENTS IN POLITICS

CELEBRATING SHIRLEY CHISHOLM, BARACK OBAMA, AND MORE

DR. ARTIKA R. TYNER
CICELY LEWIS, EXECUTIVE EDITOR

Lerner Publications ◆ Minneapolis

LETTER FROM CICELY LEWIS

Dear Reader,

As a girl, I wanted to be like Oprah Winfrey. She is a Black woman from Mississippi like me who became an award-winning actor, author, and businessperson. Oftentimes, history books leave out the accomplishments and contributions of people of color. When you see someone who looks like you and has a similar background excelling at something, it helps you to see yourself be great.

CICELY LEWIS

I created Read Woke to amplify the voices of people who are often underrepresented. These books bring to light the beauty, talent, and integrity of Black people in music, activism, sports, the arts, and other areas. As you read, think about why it's important to celebrate Black excellence and the achievements of all people regardless of race, gender, or status. How did the people mentioned succeed despite barriers placed on them? How can we use these stories to inspire others?

Black excellence is everywhere in your daily life. I hope these people inspire you to never give up and continue to let your light shine.

With gratitude,

Cicely Lewis

TABLE OF CONTENTS

Left to right: Annie Devine, Fannie Lou Hamer, and Victoria Gray lead a challenge to unseat Mississippi congresspersons in 1965.

THE IMPORTANCE OF POLITICS

During the civil rights movement in the 1950s and 1960s, Black people fought for the right to vote. Their votes would shape their community's policies and ensure equality. Civil rights leaders like Fannie Lou Hamer,

Medgar Evers, John Lewis, and Ella Baker inspired a new generation of Black people to run for office and advance toward equal rights for all.

Black politicians have lifted their voices for justice for generations. Whether it be access to quality education or affordable health care, Black politicians advocate for change.

Black people have excelled in a variety of political roles. Not every noteworthy political leader can be included in this book. But it highlights some who have shaped or are shaping the course of history.

Barack Obama makes history on January 21, 2013, when he is sworn in as the first Black US president.

On May 16, 1972, Shirley Chisholm gives a speech while running for president.

CHAPTER 1

LEADERS OF THE EXECUTIVE BRANCH

The US president has an influential role since they enforce the laws and appoint leaders to manage federal agencies. Black people have served in the White House as president and as executive leaders. They address social, economic, and political issues impacting Black communities.

DARING TO DREAM

In 1968 Shirley Chisholm made history by becoming the first Black woman elected to the US Congress. She committed to improving the lives of underserved community members. In 1972 she made history again by becoming the first Black woman to run for president on a major party ticket. She used her campaign to bring national attention to underserved people and to fight for racial and gender equality. Although she did not win the presidential election, she made history and inspired the Black political leaders who followed her steps.

Chishom (*center*) celebrates with campaign workers after being elected to Congress in 1968.

"We recall that what binds this nation together is not the colors of our skin or the tenets of our faith or the origins of our names. What makes us exceptional — what makes us American — is our allegiance to an idea articulated in a declaration made more than two centuries ago."

—PRESIDENT BARACK OBAMA, INAUGURAL ADDRESS, January 21, 2013, referring to the Declaration of Independence and people's rights

FIRST BLACK PRESIDENT

As a young lawyer, Barack Obama organized people in Chicago to better their communities. He became a state senator in 1997 and a US senator in 2005. With a message of hope for the future, he ran for president and was elected in 2008. One year into his presidency, he won the Nobel Peace Prize for his efforts in promoting unity around the world. He also fought to make health care accessible for everyone. He signed the Affordable Care Act into law in 2010. He served as president until 2017.

President Obama gives his inaugural address in 2013 at the
US Capitol after being elected to his second presidential term.

Vice President Kamala Harris swears in on January 20, 2021.

TRAILBLAZING VICE PRESIDENT

From protecting the rights of immigrants to combating hunger, Kamala Harris dedicated her career to pursuing justice. She has led with the words, "Kamala Harris, for the people." She was a district attorney, the California attorney general, and later a US senator. In 2020 she made history when she became the nation's first female, South Asian, and Black vice president.

As vice president, Harris worked on the impact of the deadly disease COVID-19 and to get people vaccinated against it. She also supported women's rights and promoted community building.

DID YOU KNOW?

In 2022 President Joe Biden appointed Karine Jean-Pierre (*below*) the White House press secretary, a spokesperson for the executive branch. The daughter of Haitian immigrants, Jean-Pierre is the first Black American and first openly LGBTQIA+ person in this role.

REFLECT

Why is it important to have diverse representation in politics?

Left to right: Secretary of State Colin Powell meeting with President George W. Bush and Secretary of Defense Donald Rumsfeld

PIONEERING SECRETARIES OF STATE

Colin Powell was a natural leader who served as a four-star general in the military and chairman of the Joint Chiefs of Staff. In 2001 he became the first Black American US secretary of state. He ran the State Department and managed the relationships between the US and other countries across the world. At the time, this was the highest civilian government leadership role ever held by a Black American.

Growing up in Birmingham, Alabama, Condoleeza Rice worked hard to reach her dream of getting a quality education. Her parents taught her that education would open windows of opportunity. Her education paid off. From 2001 to 2005, Rice worked as a national security adviser. Then she was appointed US secretary of state in 2005. She advised the president on foreign policies and helped to address global conflicts until 2009.

Civil rights activist and congressperson John Lewis served in the House of Representatives from 1987 to 2020.

CHAPTER 2

MAKING CHANGE IN THE LEGISLATIVE BRANCH

Black politicians play key roles in shaping laws and policies. They address issues such as access to education and affordable housing. Through their efforts, they help improve the daily lives of Americans.

FIGHTING FOR EQUAL OPPORTUNITIES

In 2009 Ayanna Pressley became the first woman of color elected to the Boston City Council in its one-hundred-year history. Then, in 2018, she became the first woman of color elected to Congress representing Massachusetts. Pressley is an advocate for criminal justice reform, an issue she cares strongly about since both her father and husband were incarcerated. She is concerned about the high rate of incarceration in Black communities.

Ayanna Pressley speaks at an event in 2018.

REFLECT

How do you think a person's life experiences shape their desire to lead change in their community? How have your life experiences shaped you as a leader?

Congressperson Lucy McBath speaking in 2019

ENDING GUN VIOLENCE

In 2012 Lucy McBath's son was murdered at a gas station for allegedly being in a car where the music was too loud. Her passion to end gun violence compelled her to leave her decades-long career as a flight attendant and run for office. McBath joined Congress in 2019. She works to create policies that better society. Some of the policies she supports aim to protect the rights of veterans and aid small businesses.

ADVANCING HOUSING RIGHTS

Cory Booker began fighting for the rights of tenants and fair housing in Newark, New Jersey, when he was a young lawyer. From 2006 to 2013, he was the mayor of Newark. During his time as mayor, crime decreased and affordable housing increased. Booker continues to advocate for community rights as a US senator.

Senator Cory Booker speaks during a hearing to vote on the Supreme Court nomination in 2022.

Congressperson Cori Bush gives a speech during a 2021 press conference.

Cori Bush began working in the US House of Representatives in 2021. She advocates for racial, social, and environmental justice. She also fights for housing rights. Bush experienced eviction three times. While facing houselessness, she had to live in her car with her family. During the COVID-19 pandemic, families lost their jobs and homes as they could not pay their rent. Bush wanted to see protections for renters against evictions. So she slept outside the US Capitol Building in protest. In 2021 Bush introduced an Unhoused Bill of Rights with a pledge to end houselessness by 2025.

REFLECT

The current voting age in the US is eighteen years old. Do you think the voting age should change?

DID YOU KNOW?

In 2006 lawyer Keith Ellison became the first Black American elected to Congress from Minnesota and the first Muslim to serve in Congress. He has worked to advance civil and human rights. He was elected the Minnesota attorney general in 2018 and reelected in 2022.

Attorney General Keith Ellison in 2020

CHANGE IN CONGRESS

When she was twelve, Ilhan Omar and her family fled war in Somalia and moved to the US. Omar became a US citizen in 2000. Eighteen years later, she became the first African refugee, Somali American, and woman of color elected to represent Minnesota in Congress. Omar is one of the first two Muslim women to serve in the US House of Representatives. She works to support immigrants and refugee communities.

Congressperson Ilhan Omar speaks in Washington, DC, in January 2020.

Civil rights activist and congressperson Andrew Jackson Young Jr. was mayor of Atlanta, Georgia, from 1982 to 1990.

CHAPTER 3

TAKING ON STATE-LEVEL POLITICS

Many Black people shape history in their states and hometowns. As governors and mayors, they create the policies and initiatives that impact the daily lives of community members.

Lawrence Douglas Wilder was the governor of Virginia from 1990 to 1994.

FIRST BLACK GOVERNORS

In 1989 Lawrence Douglas Wilder of Virginia was the first elected Black governor since the 1800s. During challenging economic times, he worked to keep the state budget balanced. He also helped build more mental health facilities and state parks. He supported the growth of Virginia's colleges and universities.

A Black woman has not yet served as governor in any state. Activist, politician, lawyer, and author Stacey Abrams seeks to change history. Abrams was elected to the Georgia House of Representatives in 2006. In 2018 she ran for governor of Georgia. Although she lost, she was the first Black female nominee on a major party ticket to run for governor in any state. She ran and lost again in 2022. As a politician, she promotes democracy for all.

"We know that politics can be not only discouraging, [but] it can [also] sometimes cause despair. I try to remind folks that voting isn't magic, it's medicine. It's how we treat the ills of society."

—Stacey Abrams in 2022

ONE GEORGIA
LEADERSHIP COMMITTEE
STACEYABRAMS.COM

DID YOU KNOW?

In the 2020 presidential election, two-thirds of Black women voted, putting them in third place for the highest race-gender group of voters. That year a record number of Black women ran for and won leadership roles in all levels of politics.

MAYORS MAKING A DIFFERENCE

Maynard Jackson Jr. was the first Black mayor in Atlanta, Georgia. He tried to make sure the city's Black community had equal access to employment opportunities, and he expanded the city's airport to promote tourism. This helped him prepare Atlanta to host the 1996 Olympic Summer Games. After he left office, he remained active in the Democratic Party. In 2001 he founded the African American Voters League to educate and organize voters.

Maynard Jackson Jr. in 1972

Mayor London Breed attends a news conference in 2022.

London Breed is the mayor of San Francisco, California. She works to address the needs of her community. She is the city's first Black woman and second Black person to serve in this role. She has taken a stand against houselessness by building new housing and advocates for clean air and environmental justice. She is leading efforts to build open spaces for the community. These community gathering spaces connect people with San Francisco's beauty and history.

DID YOU KNOW?

In 2016 twenty-six-year-old Michael Tubbs (*below*) became the mayor of Stockton, California. He is the youngest mayor in the city's history and the first Black mayor. Growing up, he faced many challenges, from his father being incarcerated to living in poverty. This gave him a sense of purpose to make a difference in his community.

Women voting in 2020

FUTURE POLITICAL CHANGE

Black people continue making strides in politics. They lift their voices to address the needs of their community. They create policies that foster equity and fairness. Through their advocacy, they create new pathways for justice and freedom.

REFLECT

What are some key issues that you would like to see changed in your community?

GLOSSARY

advocate: to speak or act in favor of something

eviction: removing a tenant from a property

executive: the branch of government that oversees and executes the law

immigrant: a person that moves to another country

incarceration: being in prison or jail

justice: doing what is fair or right

legislature: the branch of the government that focuses on creating laws and policies

policy: a set of rules proposed by the government

refugee: a person who leaves their country due to war or other challenges

tenant: a person or group that lives in a rented property

SOURCE NOTES

8 Barack Obama, "Inaugural Address by President Barack Obama," White House, January 21, 2013, https://obamawhitehouse.archives.gov/the-press-office/2013/01/21/inaugural-address-president-barack-obama.

10 "Kamala Harris: The Vice President," White House, accessed July 28, 2022, https://www.whitehouse.gov/administration/vice-president-harris/.

23 Nashia Baker, "Stacey Abrams Says Voting Is the Best Way to Treat the Ills of Society: It 'Isn't Magic, It's Medicine,'" *People*, May 13, 2022, https://people.com/politics/stacey-abrams-voting-treat-ills-society-isnt-magic-its-medicine-culturecon-atlanta/.

READ WOKE READING LIST

Black Americans in Congress
https://history.house.gov/baic/

Britannica Kids: Colin Powell
https://kids.britannica.com/kids/article/Colin-Powell/353664

Brown, Tameka Fryer. *Not Done Yet: Shirley Chisholm's Fight for Change*. Minneapolis: Millbrook Press, 2022.

Cherry-Paul, Sonja. *Stamped (for Kids): Racism, Antiracism, and You*. Adapted from Jason Reynolds, *Stamped: Racism, Antiracism and You*. A remix of Ibram X. Kendi, *Stamped from the Beginning*. New York: Little, Brown, 2021.

Grimes, Nikki. *Kamala Harris: Rooted in Justice*. New York: Atheneum Books for Young Readers, 2020.

"History of Women of Color in U.S. Politics"
https://cawp.rutgers.edu/history-women-color-us-politics

National Geographic Kids: African American Heroes
https://kids.nationalgeographic.com/history/topic/african-american-heroes

Obama, Barack. *Dreams from My Father (Adapted for Young Adults): A Story of Race and Inheritance*. New York: Delacorte, 2021.

INDEX

PHOTO ACKNOWLEDGMENTS

Image credits: Dick Strobel/AP Images, p. 4; Pablo Martinez Monsivais/AP Images, p. 5; Richard Drew/AP Images, p. 6; File/AP Images, p. 7; Mark Gail/Tribune News Service/Getty Images, p. 9; Gabrielle Lurie/The San Francisco Chronicle via Getty Images, p. 10; Susan Walsh/AP Images, p. 11; Brooks Kraft/CORBIS/Corbis/Getty Images, p. 12; Brooks Kraft LLC/Corbis/Getty Images, p. 13; Jeff Hutchens/Getty Images, p. 14; Christopher Evans/MediaNews Group/Boston Herald/Getty Images, p. 15; Jose Luis Magana-Pool/Getty Images, p. 16; Anna Moneymaker/Getty Images, p. 17; Sipa USA/Alamy Stock Photo, p. 18; Scott Olson/Getty Images, p. 19; JIM WATSON/AFP/Getty Images, p. 20; Bettmann/Getty Images, p. 21; Rob Crandall/Alamy Stock Photo, p. 22; Dustin Chambers/Bloomberg/Getty Images, p. 23; Bachrach/Getty Images, p. 24; Santiago Mejia/The San Francisco Chronicle/Getty Images, p. 25; REUTERS/Alamy Stock Photo, p. 26; Paul Hennessy/NurPhoto/Getty Images, p. 27.

Cover: Glasshouse Images/Alamy Stock Photo, (Shirley Chisholm); Oliver Contreras/Sipa USA/AP Images, (Barack Obama).

This book is dedicated to Stacey Abrams. She is a trailblazer for justice and champion for democracy.

Lerner Publications Company
An imprint of Lerner Publishing Group, Inc.
241 First Avenue North
Minneapolis, MN 55401 USA

For reading levels and more information, look up this title at www.lernerbooks.com.

Main body text set in Aptifer Sans LT Pro.
Typeface provided by Linotype AG.

Editor: Brianna Kaiser
Lerner team: Martha Kranes

Library of Congress Cataloging-in-Publication Data

Names: Tyner, Artika R., author.
Title: Black achievements in politics : celebrating Shirley Chisholm, Barack Obama, and more / Dr. Artika R. Tyner.
Other titles: Celebrating Shirley Chisholm, Barack Obama, and more
Description: Minneapolis : Lerner Publications, [2024] | Series: Black excellence project (Read woke books) | Includes bibliographical references and index. | Audience: Ages 9–14 | Audience: Grades 4–6
Identifiers: LCCN 2022033558 (print) | LCCN 2022033559 (ebook) | ISBN 9781728486604 (lib. bdg.) | ISBN 9781728496306 (eb pdf)
Subjects: LCSH: African American politicians—Biography—Juvenile literature. | Politicians—United States—Biography—Juvenile literature. | African Americans—Politics and government—Juvenile literature. | African American civil rights workers—Biography—Juvenile literature. | Civil rights workers—Biography—Juvenile literature.
Classification: LCC E185.96 .T96 2024 (print) | LCC E185.96 (ebook) | DDC 920.0092/96073 [B]—dc23/eng/20221206

LC record available at https://lccn.loc.gov/2022033558
LC ebook record available at https://lccn.loc.gov/2022033559

Manufactured in the United States of America
1-52590-50764-12/15/2022